Table Of Contents

Introduction

Overview of the book

"Building Wealth Legally: Harnessing the Power of Tax Shelters as an Individual" is a comprehensive guide designed to empower individuals with the knowledge and strategies needed to legally minimize their tax liabilities and build wealth through the effective use of tax shelters. This book is specifically tailored to appeal to individuals who are interested in understanding the intricacies of tax shelters and shell companies, as well as those seeking offshore tax shelter options.

In this subchapter, we will provide you with an overview of the book's content, highlighting the key topics and concepts that will be covered throughout the chapters. Our aim is to equip you with the necessary information and tools to make informed decisions regarding tax shelters, while ensuring compliance with the law.

The first section of the book delves into the world of tax shelters, explaining their purpose and benefits. We explore the various types of tax shelters available to individuals, including real estate investments, retirement accounts, and business structures. By understanding the different options, you can identify the tax shelters that align with your financial goals and personal circumstances.

Next, we turn our attention to the intriguing topic of shell companies. We delve into the world of shell companies, providing a comprehensive overview of what they are, how they operate, and their potential benefits. We explore the legal and ethical considerations surrounding shell companies, offering insights into how they can be harnessed effectively within the bounds of the law.

Finally, we address the increasingly popular concept of offshore tax shelters for individuals. We provide a detailed examination of the advantages and challenges associated with offshore tax shelters, including the potential tax savings and the legal and regulatory landscape. We also highlight the key considerations individuals need to keep in mind when exploring offshore tax shelter options.

Throughout the book, we provide practical examples, case studies, and expert insights to help you navigate the complex world of tax shelters as an individual. Our goal is to empower you with the knowledge and strategies to make informed decisions that align with your financial goals while maintaining compliance with tax laws.

Whether you are a seasoned investor looking to optimize your tax strategy or a novice seeking to understand the basics of tax shelters and shell companies, "Building Wealth Legally: Harnessing the Power of Tax Shelters as an Individual" is your comprehensive guide to achieving financial success while staying within the legal boundaries.

Importance of building wealth legally

In today's fast-paced and highly competitive world, the desire to build wealth has become a common aspiration for individuals from all walks of life. However, it is crucial to emphasize that wealth creation should always be pursued through legal means. This subchapter aims to highlight the importance of building wealth legally and the potential pitfalls of engaging in illegal or unethical practices.

One of the most significant reasons for building wealth legally is the preservation of one's reputation and integrity. Engaging in illegal activities to accumulate wealth can lead to severe consequences, both personally and professionally. The repercussions can include legal penalties, damaged relationships, and a tarnished reputation that may take years to rebuild. By choosing to build wealth legally, individuals can safeguard their credibility and maintain the trust of their peers, clients, and business partners.

Moreover, building wealth legally provides long-term stability and security. While illegal practices may offer quick and substantial gains, they often come with a high risk of exposure and subsequent loss. On the other hand, legal wealth-building strategies, such as investing in tax shelters and utilizing shell companies, offer individuals the opportunity to grow their assets in a secure and sustainable manner. These legitimate avenues provide the necessary protection and compliance with laws and regulations, ensuring that individuals can enjoy their wealth without the constant fear of legal repercussions.

It is also essential to consider the social and ethical implications of wealth accumulation. Building wealth legally contributes to the overall well-being of society by ensuring that taxes are paid, funding public services, and supporting economic growth. Engaging in illegal practices, such as offshore tax shelters, not only deprives governments of their rightful revenue but also widens the wealth gap and hampers the development of a fair and equitable society.

Lastly, building wealth legally allows individuals to pass down their assets to future generations with confidence. By following legal procedures and utilizing tax-efficient strategies, individuals can effectively plan their estate and ensure that their wealth is distributed according to their wishes. This ensures the financial stability and prosperity of their loved ones, while also setting a positive example for the next generation to follow.

In conclusion, the importance of building wealth legally cannot be overstated. By choosing to accumulate wealth through legal means, individuals can protect their reputation, achieve long-term stability, contribute to society, and secure a prosperous future for themselves and their loved ones. Embracing legal wealth-building strategies, such as tax shelters and shell companies, allows individuals to harness the power of legitimate avenues while enjoying the benefits of their hard-earned wealth.

Understanding the power of tax shelters

Tax shelters are an essential tool for individuals looking to legally minimize their tax liabilities. By taking advantage of various tax strategies and structures, individuals can significantly reduce their tax burden and increase their wealth. In this subchapter, we will delve into the concept of tax shelters, their benefits, and how individuals can harness their power to build wealth legally.

Tax shelters refer to legal methods and strategies that individuals can use to reduce their taxable income and ultimately pay less in taxes. These strategies range from utilizing deductions and credits to investing in specific assets or utilizing certain financial structures. The primary goal of tax shelters is to legally minimize tax liabilities while maximizing wealth creation and preservation.

One key aspect of tax shelters is understanding the difference between tax avoidance and tax evasion. Tax avoidance is the legal utilization of tax shelters and strategies to reduce taxes, whereas tax evasion is the illegal act of intentionally not paying taxes owed. It is crucial for individuals to understand the distinction and ensure they adhere to all tax laws and regulations.

There are various types of tax shelters available to individuals, each with its own advantages and considerations. For example, investing in retirement accounts such as 401(k)s or IRAs can provide tax-deferred growth and tax-deductible contributions. Real estate investments can offer depreciation deductions, while municipal bonds can provide tax-exempt income. Offshore tax shelters can also be utilized, but individuals must carefully navigate the legal and regulatory requirements to avoid any potential pitfalls.

One popular tax shelter strategy is the use of shell companies. By structuring a business or investment using a shell company, individuals can separate their personal assets from their business activities, potentially reducing their overall tax liability. However, it is essential to understand the legal and ethical implications of using shell companies and ensure compliance with all applicable laws and regulations.

Offshore tax shelters are another avenue individuals can explore to reduce their tax liabilities. These shelters involve establishing accounts or entities in foreign jurisdictions with favorable tax laws. While offshore tax shelters can provide tax advantages, individuals must be mindful of the legal and reporting requirements associated with such structures to avoid any legal repercussions.

In conclusion, tax shelters are powerful tools that individuals can utilize to legally minimize their tax burdens and build wealth. Understanding the various types of tax shelters, their benefits, and the legal and regulatory requirements is crucial for individuals looking to take advantage of these strategies. By harnessing the power of tax shelters, individuals can optimize their tax situation, preserve their wealth, and achieve their financial goals.

Chapter 1: Understanding Tax Shelters

Definition and types of tax shelters

In the complex world of finance and wealth management, understanding the concept of tax shelters is crucial for individuals seeking to legally minimize their tax liabilities. Tax shelters are legal strategies or structures that allow individuals to reduce their taxable income, thus reducing the amount of tax they owe to the government. These shelters can take various forms, each with its own advantages and considerations. In this subchapter, we will explore the definition and types of tax shelters, shedding light on the strategies individuals can employ to build wealth legally.

A tax shelter can be broadly defined as any legal method individuals use to reduce their taxable income, allowing them to pay less in taxes. These shelters are typically designed to take advantage of specific provisions in the tax code, providing individuals with legitimate means to minimize their tax burdens. It is important to note that while tax shelters are legal, engaging in illegal tax evasion practices is strictly prohibited and can lead to severe consequences.

There are several types of tax shelters that individuals can consider, depending on their financial goals, risk tolerance, and legal considerations. The most commonly used tax shelters include retirement accounts, such as individual retirement accounts (IRAs) and 401(k) plans, which offer individuals the opportunity to contribute pre-tax income, thus reducing their current taxable income. Investments in real estate, such as rental properties or real estate investment trusts (REITs), can also serve as tax shelters, as they often offer tax deductions on mortgage interest, property taxes, and depreciation.

Moreover, individuals can utilize offshore tax shelters to legally minimize their tax obligations. Offshore tax shelters are financial accounts or entities located in foreign jurisdictions that offer favorable tax treatment. These shelters can include offshore bank accounts, trusts, or shell companies, which can help individuals protect their assets, reduce taxation, and enhance privacy. However, it is important to note that offshore tax shelters have come under increased scrutiny in recent years, and individuals must carefully navigate the legal and compliance requirements associated with them to ensure they remain within the bounds of the law.

Understanding tax shelters and their various forms is essential for individuals looking to optimize their financial strategies. By employing these legal and legitimate methods, individuals can reduce their tax liabilities, protect their wealth, and build a solid financial foundation. However, it is crucial to seek professional advice from tax experts and financial advisors who specialize in tax planning. These professionals can offer guidance tailored to individual circumstances, ensuring compliance with tax laws while maximizing the benefits of tax shelters.

Benefits and limitations of tax shelters

Tax shelters are powerful tools that individuals can utilize to legally reduce their tax liabilities and build wealth. However, it is crucial to understand both the benefits and limitations of tax shelters in order to make informed decisions about their implementation. In this subchapter, we will explore the advantages and drawbacks of utilizing tax shelters as an individual.

Benefits of Tax Shelters:
1. Tax Savings: One of the primary advantages of tax shelters is the ability to legally minimize tax liabilities. By strategically investing in tax-advantaged assets or utilizing deductions, individuals can reduce the amount of taxable income, leading to significant savings.

2. Wealth Accumulation: Tax shelters provide individuals with opportunities to grow their wealth over time. Investments made within tax shelters, such as individual retirement accounts (IRAs) or 401(k) plans, can benefit from compounding returns, allowing individuals to accumulate substantial wealth for retirement or other financial goals.

3. Asset Protection: Certain tax shelters, such as offshore trusts or family limited partnerships, offer individuals a level of asset protection. By placing assets in these structures, individuals can shield them from potential legal claims or creditors, ensuring the preservation of their wealth.

4. Estate Planning: Tax shelters can also play a crucial role in estate planning. Through the use of trusts or gifting strategies, individuals can transfer assets to future generations while minimizing estate taxes, ensuring the smooth transfer of wealth.

Limitations of Tax Shelters:
1. Complexity and Compliance: Tax shelters often involve complex legal and financial structures that require professional guidance. Individuals must ensure full compliance with tax laws and regulations to avoid penalties or legal consequences.

2. Initial Costs and Risks: Some tax shelters, such as offshore investments or real estate ventures, may require significant upfront costs and carry inherent risks. Individuals must carefully evaluate the potential returns and associated risks before committing to these investments.

3. Limited Accessibility: Certain tax shelters, such as those involving shell companies or offshore accounts, may have strict eligibility criteria or be available only to high-net-worth individuals. This limited accessibility can restrict the options for individuals with lower incomes or assets.

4. Changing Tax Laws: Tax laws are subject to frequent changes, which can impact the effectiveness of tax shelters. Individuals must stay informed and adapt their strategies accordingly to ensure continued benefits.

In conclusion, tax shelters offer individuals numerous benefits, including tax savings, wealth accumulation, asset protection, and estate planning opportunities. However, they also come with limitations such as complexity, compliance requirements, initial costs, and changing tax laws. It is essential for individuals to carefully evaluate these benefits and limitations, seek professional advice when necessary, and make informed decisions to harness the power of tax shelters effectively.

Common misconceptions about tax shelters

Tax shelters have long been a topic of intrigue and misunderstanding among individuals looking to legally minimize their tax liabilities. In this subchapter, we aim to debunk some of the common misconceptions surrounding tax shelters, shedding light on their true nature and benefits.

Misconception #1: Tax shelters are illegal.
This is perhaps the most prevalent misconception about tax shelters. While some tax shelters have been associated with illegal activities in the past, it is important to differentiate between legal and illegal practices. There are numerous legitimate tax shelters available to individuals that comply with all applicable laws and regulations. By understanding the legitimate options, individuals can harness the power of tax shelters to their advantage.

Misconception #2: Tax shelters are only for the wealthy.
Another common misconception is that tax shelters are reserved for the rich and affluent. In reality, tax shelters can benefit individuals from all income levels. While certain tax shelters may have higher entry thresholds, there are several options available to individuals looking to save on taxes. From retirement accounts and real estate investments to education savings plans, there are numerous avenues for individuals to take advantage of tax benefits.

Misconception #3: Tax shelters are complex and require extensive knowledge. While some tax shelters can be intricate, many options are straightforward and accessible to individuals with basic financial literacy. By understanding the fundamentals and working closely with tax professionals, individuals can effectively navigate tax shelters without getting overwhelmed. This subchapter will provide a simplified overview of various tax shelters, making it easier for individuals to comprehend and implement them.

Misconception #4: Offshore tax shelters are only for hiding money. Offshore tax shelters have often been associated with illegal activities and hiding wealth. However, it is essential to note that not all offshore tax shelters are created equal. Many legitimate offshore tax shelters are designed to provide individuals with legal tax advantages, such as lower tax rates or asset protection. By understanding the legal requirements and regulations associated with offshore tax shelters, individuals can utilize them effectively and responsibly.

In conclusion, tax shelters are a valuable tool for individuals to legally minimize their tax liabilities. By dispelling these common misconceptions about tax shelters, individuals can make informed decisions and explore the various options available to them. Understanding the true nature and benefits of tax shelters is key to building wealth legally and harnessing their power to one's advantage.

Chapter 2: Legalities of Tax Shelters

The legality of tax shelters

Title: The Legality of Tax Shelters: A Comprehensive Guide for Individuals

Introduction:
In this subchapter, we delve into the intricate world of tax shelters and explore their legality. As an individual looking to build wealth legally, understanding the nuances of tax shelters is crucial. We aim to provide you with a comprehensive overview, dispel common myths, and highlight the importance of compliant tax practices. By the end, you'll be equipped with the knowledge needed to navigate tax shelter options effectively.

Understanding Tax Shelters:
Tax shelters are legitimate strategies used to reduce an individual's tax liability legally. These shelters primarily involve investments or financial arrangements that provide tax benefits, such as deductions or credits. However, it is vital to distinguish between legal tax shelters and illegal tax evasion schemes. Engaging in fraudulent practices can have severe consequences, including fines and criminal charges.

Legitimate Tax Shelters:
Various legal tax shelters exist, including retirement plans, real estate investments, and education savings accounts. These shelters are designed to incentivize individuals to save, invest, and contribute to the economy. By taking advantage of these opportunities, individuals can lower their taxable income and generate long-term wealth.

Offshore Tax Shelters:
Offshore tax shelters have gained attention due to their potential to minimize tax obligations. While these shelters are legal, it's crucial to ensure compliance with relevant regulations and reporting requirements. Failure to disclose offshore assets can result in significant penalties. We explore the benefits and

potential pitfalls of offshore tax shelters, empowering you to make informed decisions.

Shell Companies and Tax Shelters:
Shell companies, often associated with tax evasion and money laundering, deserve scrutiny. While some individuals may misuse shell companies to avoid taxes, not all shell companies are illegitimate. We shed light on the distinguishing factors between legitimate and illicit shell companies, emphasizing the importance of transparency and legal compliance.

Compliance and Transparency:
Operating within the bounds of the law is paramount when utilizing tax shelters. Complying with tax regulations ensures not only your financial security but also contributes to a fair and sustainable tax system. We provide insights into the reporting obligations and compliance requirements for tax shelters, helping you mitigate risks and maintain a clean financial record.

Conclusion:
Understanding the legality of tax shelters is essential for individuals seeking to build wealth legally. By grasping the differences between legal tax shelters and illegal tax evasion, you can make informed decisions to minimize your tax liability while staying compliant. Remember, compliance and transparency are the cornerstones of a successful tax strategy, ensuring a secure financial future for individuals and a fair tax system for society as a whole.

Compliance with tax laws and regulations

In order to effectively build and protect your wealth, it is crucial to understand and comply with tax laws and regulations. This subchapter will provide you with valuable insights on the importance of tax compliance, as well as strategies to legally harness the power of tax shelters as an individual.

Tax compliance is not only a legal obligation but also a moral responsibility. By adhering to tax laws and regulations, you contribute to the overall development of your country and ensure a fair and equitable society. Moreover, non-compliance can result in severe penalties, fines, and even criminal charges. Therefore, it is essential to stay informed and updated on any changes in tax laws that may affect you.

One powerful tool available to individuals for legally minimizing tax liabilities is the use of tax shelters. Tax shelters are legal structures that help individuals lower their tax obligations by taking advantage of various deductions, credits, and exemptions allowed by the tax code. Understanding the intricacies of tax shelters can significantly impact your financial well-being.

This subchapter will delve into the world of tax shelters and provide you with a comprehensive understanding of their benefits and limitations. We will explore different types of tax shelters, such as individual retirement accounts (IRAs), 401(k) plans, and health savings accounts (HSAs), among others. By utilizing these tax shelters, you can effectively reduce your taxable income and maximize your savings.

Additionally, we will discuss the concept of shell companies and their role in tax planning. Shell companies, when used within legal boundaries, can provide individuals with opportunities to optimize their tax liabilities and protect their assets. We will explore the benefits and risks associated with shell companies, including the importance of transparency and compliance in their usage.

Lastly, we will explore offshore tax shelters for individuals. Offshore tax shelters, when properly structured and reported, can offer individuals significant tax advantages. However, it is crucial to understand the legal framework surrounding offshore tax shelters and ensure compliance with reporting requirements to avoid any legal consequences.

By embracing tax compliance and harnessing the power of tax shelters as an individual, you can build and protect your wealth legally. This subchapter will equip you with the knowledge and strategies needed to navigate the complex world of tax laws and regulations, allowing you to make informed decisions that align with your financial goals.

Risks and consequences of illegal tax shelters

In this subchapter, we will explore the risks and consequences associated with engaging in illegal tax shelters. While tax shelters can be a legitimate and effective tool for individuals to minimize their tax liabilities, it is crucial to understand the potential pitfalls and legal ramifications that can arise from engaging in illegal activities.

Illegal tax shelters refer to schemes or strategies that intentionally evade tax laws and regulations. These activities may involve the use of shell companies, offshore accounts, or other deceptive practices to hide income, assets, or transactions from tax authorities. While the allure of reducing tax obligations may be tempting, individuals must be aware of the severe consequences that can result from participating in these illegal activities.

One of the primary risks associated with illegal tax shelters is the potential for criminal prosecution. Tax authorities have become increasingly sophisticated in detecting and investigating these schemes, leading to criminal charges and hefty penalties for offenders. Individuals found guilty of tax evasion can face substantial fines, imprisonment, or a combination of both. These consequences not only carry a financial burden but can also damage one's reputation and personal and professional relationships.

Another risk of engaging in illegal tax shelters is the ongoing stress and anxiety that individuals may experience. Living with the constant fear of being caught by tax authorities can take a toll on one's mental and emotional well-being. The pressure of maintaining complex financial structures and managing the associated risks can lead to sleepless nights and a diminished quality of life.

Furthermore, the consequences of participating in illegal tax shelters extend beyond legal ramifications. Individuals may face reputational damage, loss of business opportunities, and strained relationships with family, friends, and colleagues. The negative perception associated with tax evasion can tarnish one's personal and professional brand, making it difficult to regain trust and credibility.

To avoid the risks and consequences of illegal tax shelters, individuals are encouraged to seek professional advice from tax experts and financial planners who specialize in legal and ethical tax planning strategies. Understanding the tax laws and regulations governing your jurisdiction is essential to ensure compliance and minimize tax liabilities without resorting to illegal activities.

In conclusion, while tax shelters can be a valuable tool for individuals to legally reduce their tax obligations, engaging in illegal tax shelters can have severe consequences. The risks of criminal prosecution, financial penalties, reputational damage, and emotional distress far outweigh any potential benefits. It is important for individuals to prioritize ethical and legal tax planning strategies to build and protect their wealth while maintaining their integrity.

Chapter 3: Exploring Shell Companies

Understanding shell companies

A shell company is a legal entity that exists solely on paper and has no active business operations. It is often created for the purpose of holding assets, conducting financial transactions, or minimizing tax liabilities. Shell companies are a popular tool used by individuals to legally build wealth and protect their assets. In this subchapter, we will delve into the intricacies of shell companies, their benefits, and their relevance to tax shelters for individuals.

First and foremost, it is important to understand the concept of a tax shelter. A tax shelter refers to any legal strategy that allows individuals to minimize their tax liabilities and maximize their after-tax income. Shell companies play a significant role in tax sheltering by providing individuals with a means to legally reduce their tax burdens.

One of the key advantages of using a shell company is the ability to hold and protect assets. By transferring assets to a shell company, individuals can separate their personal wealth from their business or investment activities, providing an additional layer of protection against liabilities and legal claims. Additionally, shell companies can be used to hold liquid assets, such as cash or investments, which can be shielded from taxes or lawsuits.

Another benefit of shell companies is their ability to facilitate financial transactions. Through a shell company, individuals can engage in complex financial operations, such as mergers and acquisitions, without revealing their true identities or intentions. This level of anonymity can be advantageous in negotiating deals, protecting sensitive information, and maintaining privacy.

Furthermore, shell companies can be utilized for tax planning purposes. By establishing a shell company in a jurisdiction with favorable tax laws, individuals can legally reduce their tax liabilities. Offshore tax shelters are particularly popular for individuals seeking to minimize their tax burdens, as they often offer low or zero tax rates on certain types of income. However, it is crucial to note that proper compliance with tax regulations and reporting requirements is essential to avoid any legal issues.

In conclusion, shell companies are powerful tools for individuals looking to build wealth legally and harness the benefits of tax shelters. By understanding the intricacies of shell companies, individuals can effectively protect their assets, conduct financial transactions, and minimize their tax liabilities. However, it is important to consult with professional advisors and ensure compliance with legal and tax regulations to maximize the benefits of using shell companies as part of a comprehensive tax planning strategy.

Uses and benefits of shell companies

Subchapter: Uses and Benefits of Shell Companies

In today's complex financial landscape, individuals are constantly seeking ways to optimize their wealth-building strategies while remaining compliant with the ever-evolving tax laws. One often overlooked avenue for achieving these goals is through the use of shell companies. In this subchapter, we will explore the various uses and benefits of shell companies, shedding light on how they can be harnessed legally to enhance your financial success.

1. Asset Protection: One of the primary advantages of utilizing a shell company is the ability to safeguard your assets. By placing your assets under the ownership of a separate legal entity, you create a barrier between your personal wealth and potential creditors or litigants. This provides a layer of protection, shielding your valuable assets from legal disputes, bankruptcies, or other unforeseen circumstances.

2. Privacy and Confidentiality: Shell companies offer individuals the opportunity to maintain a certain level of privacy and confidentiality in their financial affairs. By structuring your investments and assets through a shell company, you can shield your personal information, making it harder for prying eyes to connect your wealth to your identity.

3. Tax Optimization: Shell companies, when used correctly, can be a powerful tool for optimizing your tax liability. By establishing a shell company in a jurisdiction with favorable tax laws, you can legally minimize your tax burden. Through careful planning and strategic structuring, you can take advantage of tax deductions, exemptions, and incentives that are otherwise inaccessible to individuals.

4. International Expansion: For individuals looking to expand their business interests internationally, shell companies can offer a convenient and flexible solution. By establishing a presence in offshore jurisdictions, you can benefit from lower taxation, reduced regulatory requirements, and access to global markets. Shell companies can serve as a gateway to international business opportunities, helping you diversify your income streams and protect your wealth.

5. Succession Planning: Shell companies also play a vital role in effective succession planning. By transferring assets and ownership of your business to a shell company, you can ensure a smooth transition of wealth to your heirs while minimizing estate taxes and potential disputes among family members.

It is important to note that while shell companies can provide numerous benefits, their usage must be within the boundaries of the law. Transparency and compliance with tax regulations are crucial. This subchapter aims to provide you with a comprehensive understanding of the potential uses and benefits of shell companies, empowering you to make informed decisions about your wealth-building strategies and tax planning. Remember, the key to harnessing the power of shell companies lies in understanding the legal frameworks and seeking professional guidance to ensure your financial activities remain above board and in line with the relevant regulations.

Legitimate purposes of shell companies in tax planning

In the complex world of tax planning, shell companies have gained a reputation for being used solely as vehicles for tax evasion and illicit activities. However, it is essential to recognize that shell companies can also serve legitimate purposes in tax planning when used appropriately and within the boundaries of the law. This subchapter aims to shed light on the legitimate uses of shell companies in tax planning, providing individuals with a comprehensive understanding of their potential benefits.

1. Asset Protection: One of the primary legitimate purposes of shell companies is asset protection. By holding assets within a shell company, individuals can safeguard their wealth from potential risks, such as lawsuits or creditors. This strategy is particularly beneficial for high-net-worth individuals who want to shield their assets while maintaining control over them.

2. Privacy and Confidentiality: Another legitimate reason for utilizing shell companies is to ensure privacy and maintain confidentiality. In an increasingly interconnected world, individuals may wish to keep their financial affairs discreet. A shell company can help achieve this by acting as an intermediary, preventing direct association between the individual and their assets.

3. International Business Ventures: Shell companies can facilitate international business ventures by acting as a subsidiary or holding company. They can help streamline cross-border transactions, manage foreign investments, and reduce tax liabilities legally. For individuals engaged in global business activities, shell companies provide a practical solution for organizing and optimizing their international operations.

4. Succession Planning: Shell companies can also be utilized as part of a comprehensive succession plan. By transferring assets to a shell company, individuals can ensure a smooth transition of wealth to future generations while minimizing tax implications. This strategy allows individuals to

maintain control over their assets during their lifetime, while also ensuring their intended beneficiaries receive the benefits in the future.

It is crucial to note that while shell companies can serve legitimate purposes in tax planning, their misuse for illegal activities remains a concern. As individuals explore the potential benefits of shell companies, they must adhere to the legal and ethical guidelines governing their use. Seeking professional advice from tax experts and legal advisors is strongly recommended to ensure compliance with the relevant laws and regulations.

By understanding the legitimate purposes of shell companies in tax planning, individuals can make informed decisions about incorporating them into their financial strategies. When used responsibly and within legal boundaries, shell companies can offer valuable tools for asset protection, privacy, international business ventures, and succession planning.

Chapter 4: Setting Up a Shell Company

Steps to establish a shell company legally

In this subchapter, we will discuss the steps that individuals can take to establish a shell company legally. A shell company is a non-operational entity that is primarily used for holding assets, conducting financial transactions, or reducing tax liabilities. While some people may associate shell companies with illegal activities, it is important to note that they can be established and utilized legally by individuals for various purposes, including tax planning and asset protection.

1. Understand the Purpose: Before establishing a shell company, it is crucial to have a clear understanding of the purpose behind it. Determine whether you need a shell company for asset protection, tax planning, or any other legitimate reason. This will help you structure the company accordingly and ensure compliance with relevant legal regulations.

2. Seek Legal Advice: Consulting with a qualified tax attorney or legal professional specializing in tax shelters and shell companies is highly recommended. They can guide you through the legal process and ensure that your shell company is established in compliance with all applicable laws and regulations.

3. Select an Appropriate Jurisdiction: Choose a jurisdiction that offers favorable tax and legal frameworks for establishing a shell company. Offshore jurisdictions are often popular choices due to their lenient tax laws and strict privacy regulations. However, it is essential to consider the reputation and stability of the chosen jurisdiction to ensure long-term viability.

4. Register the Company: Once you have selected a jurisdiction, register your shell company by filing the necessary documents and paying the required fees.

This process typically involves providing basic information about the company, such as its name, registered address, and initial capital.

5. Appoint Directors and Shareholders: Depending on the jurisdiction, you may need to appoint directors and shareholders for your shell company. It is important to carefully select individuals who are trustworthy and understand their roles and responsibilities.

6. Maintain Proper Documentation: To establish the legitimacy of your shell company, maintain accurate and up-to-date documentation, including shareholder agreements, board meeting minutes, and financial records. This will help demonstrate that your shell company is operating transparently and in compliance with legal requirements.

7. Comply with Reporting Obligations: Be aware of and comply with all reporting obligations imposed by the chosen jurisdiction. This may include annual financial statements, tax returns, and other relevant disclosures. Failing to meet these obligations can lead to legal consequences and tarnish the reputation of your shell company.

Remember, the establishment and operation of a shell company should always be done legally and within the boundaries of applicable laws and regulations. It is crucial to seek professional advice and ensure compliance at all times. By following these steps, individuals can harness the power of shell companies as legitimate vehicles for wealth building, tax planning, and asset protection.

Choosing the right jurisdiction for a shell company

When it comes to building wealth legally, one of the powerful tools at your disposal is the creation of a shell company. A shell company, also known as a non-trading or inactive company, is a legal entity that is formed primarily for holding assets, reducing tax liabilities, and providing privacy and asset protection. However, the success of your shell company largely depends on choosing the right jurisdiction in which to establish it.

Selecting the right jurisdiction for your shell company is crucial, as it can significantly impact the tax benefits, legal protections, and overall effectiveness of your wealth-building strategy. Here are some key considerations to keep in mind when deciding on the jurisdiction for your shell company:

1. Tax Benefits: Different jurisdictions offer varying tax advantages for shell companies. Some jurisdictions have low or no corporate taxes, while others may have preferential tax regimes for certain industries. Understanding the tax implications of each jurisdiction is essential to maximize your tax savings and overall profitability.

2. Legal and Regulatory Environment: Evaluate the legal and regulatory framework of potential jurisdictions. Look for jurisdictions that have strong legal protections, political stability, and a well-established legal system. This will ensure that your assets are safeguarded and that your shell company operates in a secure and predictable environment.

3. Privacy and Confidentiality: Maintaining privacy and confidentiality is often a priority for individuals considering a shell company. Some jurisdictions have stringent regulations regarding the disclosure of company ownership, while others offer greater anonymity. Consider the level of privacy you require and choose a jurisdiction that aligns with your preferences.

4. Reputation and Credibility: Reputation matters, especially when it comes to offshore entities. Opt for jurisdictions that are well-regarded and have a history of being cooperative with international tax authorities. A strong reputation can help enhance the credibility of your shell company and minimize potential scrutiny from tax authorities.

5. Ease of Doing Business: Consider the ease of establishing and operating a shell company in a particular jurisdiction. Look for jurisdictions with streamlined company incorporation processes, minimal bureaucratic red tape, and a business-friendly environment. This will ensure that you can set up and manage your shell company efficiently.

Remember, choosing the right jurisdiction for your shell company is a critical step in your wealth-building journey. Seek professional advice from tax consultants, lawyers, and experts specializing in offshore tax shelters to ensure that you make an informed decision that aligns with your financial goals and risk tolerance.

In the next chapters, we will delve deeper into specific offshore tax shelters for individuals and explore the intricacies of establishing and managing a shell company in different jurisdictions. By understanding the nuances and benefits of each jurisdiction, you can leverage the power of tax shelters and shell companies to legally build and protect your wealth.

Compliance requirements for shell companies

When it comes to utilizing tax shelters and shell companies as individuals, it is important to understand and adhere to the compliance requirements set forth by regulatory authorities. While shell companies can offer significant benefits in terms of tax planning and asset protection, it is crucial to operate within the legal boundaries.

First and foremost, it is essential to establish a clear distinction between legitimate tax planning strategies and illegal tax evasion. A shell company, or an entity formed primarily for holding assets or conducting business transactions, should be set up with a genuine business purpose and not merely as a means to hide income or evade taxes. By ensuring the legitimacy of your shell company, you can navigate the complex world of tax shelters legally and ethically.

One of the key compliance requirements for shell companies is maintaining accurate and up-to-date financial records. It is imperative to keep detailed records of all financial transactions, including income, expenses, assets, and liabilities. These records should be properly organized and readily available for review by tax authorities or any other relevant regulatory bodies. Failure to maintain accurate records can result in serious penalties or even legal repercussions.

Additionally, transparency is crucial when it comes to shell companies. It is important to disclose the ownership and control structure of the company, as well as any related party transactions. This includes providing information about beneficial owners, directors, and shareholders. Compliance with anti-money laundering (AML) regulations is also paramount, as shell companies can sometimes be misused for illicit activities. Ensuring proper due diligence and Know Your Customer (KYC) procedures will help prevent any misuse and maintain a clean reputation.

Furthermore, it is important to understand and comply with the tax regulations in both the home country and the jurisdiction where the shell company is incorporated. This includes filing tax returns, paying taxes, and adhering to any reporting requirements. Seeking professional advice from tax experts who specialize in cross-border transactions can be immensely helpful in navigating the complexities of international tax laws while remaining compliant.

In conclusion, compliance requirements for shell companies are of utmost importance when utilizing tax shelters as an individual. By maintaining accurate financial records, ensuring transparency, and complying with tax regulations, individuals can effectively harness the benefits of shell companies while avoiding legal and financial pitfalls. Remember, utilizing tax shelters legally and ethically is not only beneficial for wealth building but also for maintaining a strong financial reputation.

Chapter 5: Offshore Tax Shelters for Individuals

Introduction to offshore tax shelters

In today's complex financial landscape, individuals are constantly seeking ways to legally reduce their tax liabilities while maximizing wealth accumulation. One strategy that has gained significant attention is the utilization of offshore tax shelters. These offshore tax havens offer individuals a unique opportunity to legally minimize tax burdens and protect their assets from various financial risks.

This subchapter aims to provide individuals with a comprehensive introduction to offshore tax shelters, shedding light on their benefits, potential risks, and the legal framework surrounding their use. By understanding the fundamentals of offshore tax shelters, individuals can make informed decisions to harness their power and build wealth legally.

To begin, it is crucial to define what offshore tax shelters are. Essentially, offshore tax shelters are legal structures established in foreign jurisdictions that offer favorable tax treatment to individuals. These jurisdictions, commonly known as tax havens, provide a range of incentives, such as low or zero tax rates, strict privacy laws, and asset protection measures. By utilizing these shelters, individuals can legally reduce their tax liabilities, grow their wealth, and safeguard their assets.

One of the primary benefits of offshore tax shelters is their ability to facilitate tax deferral. By shifting income or assets to these tax havens, individuals can delay paying taxes until a later date, allowing their investments to grow and compound tax-free. Furthermore, offshore tax shelters often provide individuals with increased privacy and confidentiality, as these jurisdictions have strict laws protecting the confidentiality of financial information.

However, it is essential to recognize the potential risks and legal considerations associated with offshore tax shelters. While they offer legitimate tax advantages, individuals must ensure compliance with the tax laws of their home countries. It is essential to understand the reporting requirements, disclosure obligations, and potential penalties associated with utilizing offshore tax shelters. Failing to comply with these legal obligations can result in severe consequences, including hefty fines and even criminal charges.

In this subchapter, we will explore the legal framework surrounding offshore tax shelters, discussing the key factors individuals need to consider before establishing such structures. We will also delve into the various types of offshore tax shelters available to individuals, examining their specific advantages and limitations.

By gaining a solid understanding of offshore tax shelters, individuals can navigate the complexities of these financial tools with confidence, making informed decisions that align with their wealth-building goals. With careful planning and adherence to legal obligations, offshore tax shelters can provide individuals with a powerful means to legally reduce their tax burdens and safeguard their wealth.

Benefits and drawbacks of offshore tax shelters

Offshore tax shelters have long been a topic of interest for individuals seeking to legally minimize their tax obligations. These shelters, often located in low-tax or tax haven jurisdictions, offer a range of benefits, as well as some potential drawbacks. In this subchapter, we will explore both the advantages and disadvantages of offshore tax shelters, providing individuals with a comprehensive understanding of this complex financial tool.

One of the key benefits of offshore tax shelters is the potential for significant tax savings. By establishing a legal entity in a low-tax jurisdiction, individuals can take advantage of favorable tax laws and regulations. This can result in reduced tax liability, allowing individuals to retain more of their hard-earned income. Additionally, offshore tax shelters can provide individuals with greater privacy and confidentiality, as these jurisdictions often have strict laws in place to protect the identity and financial information of investors.

Another notable advantage of offshore tax shelters is the opportunity for asset protection. In some cases, offshore jurisdictions offer strong legal frameworks that can safeguard an individual's assets from creditors or legal disputes. By holding assets in an offshore entity, individuals can shield their wealth from potential risks and uncertainties, ensuring its preservation for future generations.

However, it is important to consider the drawbacks associated with offshore tax shelters. One significant concern is the potential for increased scrutiny from tax authorities. While utilizing offshore tax shelters is legal, it is crucial to comply with all reporting requirements and disclose any offshore holdings to avoid penalties or legal consequences. Failing to do so can lead to reputational damage and a loss of financial resources.

Furthermore, offshore tax shelters may require additional administrative and legal expenses. Establishing and maintaining an offshore entity can involve complex legal procedures and ongoing compliance requirements. These costs should be carefully considered and weighed against the potential tax savings before deciding to utilize an offshore tax shelter.

Lastly, offshore tax shelters have faced criticism for facilitating tax evasion and illicit financial activities. While this is not the intention of all individuals utilizing offshore tax shelters, it is important to be aware of the potential reputational risks associated with such arrangements.

In conclusion, offshore tax shelters offer individuals the opportunity to legally reduce their tax obligations and protect their assets. However, they come with potential drawbacks such as increased scrutiny, administrative costs, and reputational risks. It is essential for individuals to thoroughly research and understand the legal and financial implications of utilizing offshore tax shelters before making any decisions.

Legal considerations when utilizing offshore tax shelters

Introduction:
In today's increasingly globalized world, individuals seeking to maximize their wealth often turn to offshore tax shelters as a means of reducing their tax liabilities. While these structures can provide significant benefits, it is crucial to understand the legal considerations involved. This subchapter delves into the legal aspects that individuals need to consider when utilizing offshore tax shelters, providing insights and guidance to ensure compliance with applicable laws and regulations.

Understanding Tax Laws and Reporting Obligations:
Utilizing offshore tax shelters requires a comprehensive understanding of both domestic and international tax laws. Individuals must be aware of their reporting obligations, including the disclosure of offshore assets and income to tax authorities. Failure to comply with these requirements can result in severe penalties and legal consequences. This subchapter provides an overview of the key reporting obligations and discusses strategies to meet these obligations effectively.

Navigating International Tax Treaties:
International tax treaties play a crucial role in determining the tax treatments individuals receive in different jurisdictions. These treaties aim to prevent double taxation and promote cooperation between countries. Understanding the provisions of relevant tax treaties is essential when utilizing offshore tax shelters. This subchapter explores the common provisions found in tax treaties and offers guidance on leveraging these agreements to maximize tax benefits legally.

Compliance with Anti-Money Laundering (AML) Regulations:
Offshore tax shelters are subject to stringent anti-money laundering regulations aimed at preventing illegal activities and ensuring transparency. Individuals utilizing these structures must comply with these regulations, including Know Your Customer (KYC) requirements and due diligence obligations. This subchapter provides an overview of AML regulations and outlines the steps individuals should take to remain compliant while utilizing offshore tax shelters.

Risk of Tax Evasion and Tax Fraud:
While offshore tax shelters can be legitimate and legal, there is a risk of individuals engaging in tax evasion or fraudulent activities. This subchapter highlights the importance of maintaining transparency, adhering to ethical practices, and avoiding any illegal activities. It also discusses the potential legal consequences individuals may face if they engage in tax evasion or tax fraud.

Conclusion:
Utilizing offshore tax shelters allows individuals to legally reduce their tax burdens. However, it is imperative to understand and navigate the legal considerations involved to ensure compliance and avoid legal complications. This subchapter provides individuals with the necessary insights, strategies, and guidance to leverage offshore tax shelters effectively and lawfully, helping them build wealth legally while staying on the right side of the law.

Chapter 6: Selecting the Right Offshore Tax Shelter

Factors to consider when choosing an offshore tax shelter

When it comes to building wealth legally, offshore tax shelters can play a significant role in minimizing tax liabilities and maximizing financial gains. However, choosing the right offshore tax shelter requires careful consideration of various factors. In this subchapter, we will explore the key factors that individuals should consider when selecting an offshore tax shelter to ensure compliance with legal regulations and maximize financial benefits.

1. Jurisdiction Selection: The choice of jurisdiction is critical when establishing an offshore tax shelter. Consider jurisdictions with favorable tax laws, political stability, and a reputable financial system. Popular options include Switzerland, the Cayman Islands, and Singapore. Research the tax laws, reporting requirements, and privacy regulations of each jurisdiction to align them with your financial goals and risk tolerance.

2. Tax Laws: Understand the tax laws of both your home country and the chosen offshore jurisdiction. Ensure that the offshore tax shelter is compliant with the tax regulations of your home country to avoid legal consequences. Seek advice from experienced tax professionals who can guide you through the complexities of international tax laws.

3. Privacy and Confidentiality: Offshore tax shelters are often chosen for their privacy benefits. Evaluate the level of privacy and confidentiality offered by the chosen jurisdiction. Look for jurisdictions with strict banking secrecy laws and regulations that protect your personal and financial information from unauthorized access or disclosure.

4. Reputation and Stability: Stability and reputation of the jurisdiction are crucial factors to consider. Choose jurisdictions with a strong financial system, political stability, and a history of respecting international agreements. Such jurisdictions are less likely to face scrutiny or changes in tax regulations that could jeopardize your offshore tax shelter.

5. Compliance and Reporting Requirements: Ensure that the chosen offshore tax shelter complies with all legal requirements and reporting obligations. Failure to adhere to reporting obligations can result in severe penalties. Understand the documentation and reporting requirements of both your home country and the offshore jurisdiction to maintain legal compliance.

6. Professional Advice: Seek guidance from experienced professionals, such as tax attorneys, accountants, and financial advisors, who specialize in international tax planning. They can help you navigate the complexities of offshore tax shelters and ensure that your financial strategies align with legal frameworks.

Remember, offshore tax shelters can provide significant benefits, but they must be established and managed within the boundaries of the law. By considering these factors, individuals can make informed decisions and harness the power of offshore tax shelters to legally build and protect their wealth.

Popular offshore tax shelter jurisdictions for individuals

In the ever-evolving world of finance, individuals are constantly seeking ways to protect and grow their wealth legally. One strategy that has gained significant attention is the use of offshore tax shelters. These jurisdictions, known for their favorable tax laws and regulations, provide individuals with opportunities to minimize their tax liabilities, protect their assets, and enhance their overall financial well-being.

There are several popular offshore tax shelter jurisdictions that individuals often consider when exploring this avenue. Each jurisdiction offers unique advantages and considerations, making it essential for individuals to understand the options available to them. In this subchapter, we will delve into some of the most popular offshore tax shelter jurisdictions for individuals.

1. Cayman Islands: Renowned for its tax-free status, the Cayman Islands is a preferred choice for individuals seeking complete tax exemption on their offshore investments. With a robust financial services industry and strict confidentiality laws, the Cayman Islands provide an attractive environment for wealth accumulation and preservation.

2. Switzerland: Known for its banking secrecy laws, Switzerland has long been a favorite destination for individuals looking to safeguard their assets. The country offers stability, a strong legal framework, and a well-established banking system, making it an ideal choice for those seeking privacy and wealth protection.

3. British Virgin Islands (BVI): The BVI is widely recognized as a popular offshore jurisdiction for individuals due to its tax neutrality and flexible corporate structures. With no capital gains or income tax, the BVI offers individuals a favorable environment for wealth accumulation and international business operations.

4. Panama: With its strategic location and favorable tax regime, Panama has emerged as a preferred choice for individuals seeking asset protection and tax optimization. Its offshore structures, including private interest foundations and bearer share corporations, provide individuals with enhanced privacy and asset diversification opportunities.

5. Luxembourg: Known for its favorable tax regime and extensive network of double taxation treaties, Luxembourg is a popular choice for individuals looking to optimize their tax liabilities while enjoying stability and asset

protection. The country's sophisticated financial services industry and strong legal framework make it an attractive destination for wealth management.

It is important to note that while these jurisdictions offer favorable tax benefits, individuals must comply with their home country's tax regulations and disclose their offshore holdings as required by law. Seeking professional advice from tax experts and legal counsel is crucial to ensure compliance and maximize the benefits of offshore tax shelters.

In conclusion, offshore tax shelter jurisdictions provide individuals with opportunities to legally minimize their tax liabilities, protect their assets, and build wealth. Understanding the advantages and considerations of popular jurisdictions such as the Cayman Islands, Switzerland, British Virgin Islands, Panama, and Luxembourg is essential for individuals looking to harness the power of offshore tax shelters for their financial well-being.

Evaluating the legitimacy and reliability of offshore tax shelters

In today's ever-evolving financial landscape, individuals are constantly seeking ways to legally minimize their tax burdens and build wealth. One strategy that has gained popularity is the use of offshore tax shelters. These financial vehicles offer a range of benefits, including reduced tax liability, asset protection, and increased privacy. However, it is crucial for individuals to evaluate the legitimacy and reliability of these offshore tax shelters before diving into them.

Legitimacy is the key factor when considering any tax shelter. It is essential to ensure that the offshore tax shelter complies with all applicable laws and regulations. Engaging in illegal tax evasion schemes can have severe consequences, including hefty fines and even criminal charges. Therefore, individuals should thoroughly research the legal framework surrounding offshore tax shelters and consult with reputable tax professionals to ensure compliance.

Reliability is another critical aspect to evaluate. Offshore tax shelters are typically established in countries that offer favorable tax environments. However, not all jurisdictions are created equal. It is imperative to consider the reputation and stability of the chosen offshore jurisdiction. Reliable tax havens have well-established legal systems, political stability, and robust financial and regulatory frameworks. These factors contribute to the overall credibility and longevity of the offshore tax shelter.

Furthermore, individuals must carefully assess the level of transparency and reporting requirements associated with the offshore tax shelter. In recent years, there has been a global push for greater transparency in financial transactions to combat money laundering and tax evasion. Therefore, it is vital to ensure that the chosen offshore tax shelter adheres to international reporting standards, such as those set by the Organization for Economic Cooperation and Development (OECD).

Additionally, individuals should consider the track record and reputation of the service providers associated with the offshore tax shelter. Reputable trustees, lawyers, and financial institutions play a crucial role in the proper functioning and management of the offshore tax shelter. Conducting due diligence on these service providers is essential to ensure their credibility and reliability.

In conclusion, offshore tax shelters can be powerful tools for individuals looking to legally minimize their tax liabilities and build wealth. However, evaluating the legitimacy and reliability of these offshore tax shelters is paramount. Individuals must ensure compliance with laws and regulations, assess the credibility of the chosen jurisdiction, consider transparency and reporting requirements, and thoroughly research the reputation of service providers. By undertaking these evaluations, individuals can confidently harness the power of offshore tax shelters to achieve their financial goals while staying within legal boundaries.

Chapter 7: Maximizing Tax Savings with Offshore Tax Shelters

Strategies for optimizing tax savings through offshore tax shelters

Introduction:

In today's increasingly complex financial landscape, individuals are constantly seeking legal ways to minimize their tax liabilities and maximize their wealth. One powerful tool in this pursuit is the use of offshore tax shelters. This subchapter aims to provide individuals with valuable strategies for optimizing tax savings through offshore tax shelters. By understanding the benefits and limitations of these structures, individuals can make informed decisions that align with their financial goals while complying with all relevant laws and regulations.

1. Understanding Offshore Tax Shelters:

Offshore tax shelters refer to legal entities established in low-tax or tax-free jurisdictions. These structures offer individuals the opportunity to reduce their tax burdens by taking advantage of favorable tax laws, exemptions, and incentives. Understanding the basics of offshore tax shelters is crucial, including the concept of a shell company, which acts as a vehicle for holding assets and generating income.

2. Selecting the Right Jurisdiction:

Choosing the appropriate offshore jurisdiction is paramount to optimizing tax savings. Factors to consider include the jurisdiction's tax laws, stability, reputation, and adherence to international tax standards. It is essential to consult with tax professionals and legal experts who specialize in offshore tax planning to ensure compliance and maximize benefits.

3. Utilizing Legal Tax Avoidance Strategies:

While tax evasion is illegal, tax avoidance is a legitimate method of reducing tax liabilities. By structuring transactions and assets within offshore tax shelters, individuals can take advantage of legal tax avoidance strategies. These may include utilizing tax treaties, capitalizing on foreign tax credits, and employing transfer pricing techniques.

4. Asset Protection and Estate Planning:
Offshore tax shelters can also serve as effective tools for asset protection and estate planning. By placing assets within these structures, individuals can shield them from potential lawsuits, creditors, or inheritance disputes. Additionally, offshore tax shelters can facilitate the seamless transfer of wealth to future generations, minimizing tax consequences along the way.

5. Staying Compliant with Tax Laws:
While offshore tax shelters offer numerous benefits, it is crucial to maintain compliance with tax laws and reporting requirements. Governments worldwide are increasingly cracking down on tax evasion and implementing stricter regulations. Individuals should ensure they understand their obligations, such as filing Foreign Bank Account Reports (FBARs) and adhering to the Common Reporting Standard (CRS).

Conclusion:
Optimizing tax savings through offshore tax shelters requires careful planning, understanding of the legal frameworks, and compliance with tax laws. By implementing the strategies discussed in this subchapter, individuals can harness the power of offshore tax shelters to build wealth legally while protecting their assets and maximizing their tax savings. However, it is important to seek professional advice to ensure compliance and adherence to all relevant regulations.

Understanding tax planning and minimizing tax liabilities

Tax planning is an essential aspect of financial management that allows individuals to legally minimize their tax liabilities. By strategically structuring their financial affairs, individuals can take advantage of various tax shelters and strategies to reduce the amount of taxes they owe, ultimately building wealth legally. This subchapter aims to provide individuals with a comprehensive understanding of tax planning and the tools available to minimize tax liabilities.

Tax planning involves careful consideration of the tax laws and regulations applicable to individuals. It requires a thorough understanding of the tax code, including deductions, credits, exemptions, and other provisions that can be utilized to reduce taxable income. By utilizing these provisions effectively, individuals can legally minimize their tax liabilities and retain more of their hard-earned money.

One of the key aspects of tax planning is the use of tax shelters. Tax shelters are legal structures or investments that provide individuals with tax benefits. They can include retirement accounts, such as individual retirement accounts (IRAs) and 401(k) plans, which offer tax advantages such as tax-deferred growth or tax-free withdrawals in retirement. Other tax shelters may include real estate investments, which provide depreciation deductions, or investments in certain industries that offer tax incentives.

Furthermore, individuals can also explore the use of shell companies and offshore tax shelters to minimize tax liabilities. While these strategies are legal, it is crucial to understand the regulations and requirements associated with them. Offshore tax shelters, for instance, may require compliance with international tax laws and reporting obligations.

To effectively implement tax planning strategies, individuals should consult with qualified tax professionals who can provide guidance tailored to their specific financial situation. These professionals can help individuals navigate the complexities of tax laws and regulations, ensuring compliance while maximizing tax benefits.

In conclusion, tax planning is a crucial aspect of financial management for individuals looking to minimize their tax liabilities and build wealth legally. By understanding the tax code, utilizing tax shelters, and seeking professional guidance, individuals can strategically structure their financial affairs to keep more of their income and invest in their future. This subchapter provides an overview of tax planning and its various tools, empowering individuals to make informed decisions and optimize their tax position.

Compliance and reporting requirements for offshore tax shelters

In today's complex financial landscape, individuals are constantly seeking legal ways to minimize their tax liabilities and maximize their wealth. One such avenue that has gained significant popularity is offshore tax shelters. These offshore tax shelters provide individuals with an opportunity to legally reduce their tax burdens by taking advantage of international tax laws and financial structures.

However, it is crucial for individuals to understand that while offshore tax shelters can be a legitimate and effective tool for wealth building, they come with stringent compliance and reporting requirements. These requirements ensure that individuals remain within the boundaries of the law and avoid any potential legal and financial consequences.

When utilizing offshore tax shelters, individuals must be aware of the reporting obligations imposed by their home country's tax authorities. Tax authorities are becoming increasingly vigilant in identifying and cracking down on tax evasion and money laundering activities associated with offshore tax shelters. Therefore, it is essential for individuals to comply with all reporting requirements to avoid penalties and legal troubles.

Typically, individuals must disclose their offshore tax shelter activities through various forms, such as FBAR (Report of Foreign Bank and Financial Accounts) and FATCA (Foreign Account Tax Compliance Act) filings. These forms require individuals to report their offshore financial holdings, income, and transactions. Failing to disclose this information can result in hefty fines, criminal charges, and reputational damage.

Furthermore, individuals must also ensure that their offshore tax shelters comply with the tax laws and regulations of both their home country and the offshore jurisdiction. This includes adhering to rules regarding residency, income sourcing, transfer pricing, and controlled foreign corporation (CFC) regulations. By ensuring compliance with these laws, individuals can maintain the legitimacy of their offshore tax shelters and mitigate any potential legal risks.

In conclusion, offshore tax shelters can be a powerful tool for individuals seeking to build wealth legally. However, it is vital to understand and fulfill the compliance and reporting requirements associated with these tax shelters. By doing so, individuals can confidently navigate the complex world of offshore tax shelters, minimize their tax liabilities, and protect their financial interests.

Chapter 8: Risks and Challenges of Offshore Tax Shelters

Common risks and challenges associated with offshore tax shelters

Offshore tax shelters have gained popularity among individuals seeking to legally minimize their tax liability. These shelters, often established in low-tax or tax-free jurisdictions, offer numerous benefits to individuals looking to protect their wealth. However, it is important to understand the potential risks and challenges that come with utilizing offshore tax shelters.

One common risk associated with offshore tax shelters is increased scrutiny from tax authorities. Governments around the world have become more aggressive in cracking down on tax evasion and aggressive tax planning strategies. As a result, individuals who utilize offshore tax shelters may face heightened scrutiny from tax authorities, potentially leading to audits and investigations. It is crucial for individuals to ensure their tax planning is legitimate and compliant with the laws of their home jurisdiction and the offshore jurisdiction where the tax shelter is established.

Another challenge individuals may face with offshore tax shelters is the complexity of the legal and regulatory frameworks involved. Offshore jurisdictions often have different tax laws, reporting requirements, and disclosure obligations compared to an individual's home country. Navigating these complex legal landscapes can be challenging, requiring individuals to seek professional advice from tax experts who specialize in international tax planning. Failure to comply with the legal and regulatory requirements of both jurisdictions can result in severe penalties and reputational damage.

Furthermore, offshore tax shelters may also pose risks related to the lack of transparency and the potential for misuse. Some individuals may use offshore tax shelters for illicit purposes, such as money laundering or hiding assets from creditors. Engaging in such activities can expose individuals to legal and reputational risks, as governments and international organizations continue to enhance their efforts to combat financial crimes and promote transparency.

Lastly, changes in tax laws and international agreements can also pose challenges for individuals utilizing offshore tax shelters. Governments may introduce new legislation or amend existing laws to target tax avoidance strategies, potentially rendering certain tax shelters less effective or even illegal. Staying informed about changes in tax regulations and maintaining regular communication with tax advisors is crucial to ensure that offshore tax planning strategies remain compliant and effective.

In conclusion, offshore tax shelters offer individuals the opportunity to legally minimize their tax liability. However, it is important to be aware of the risks and challenges associated with these tax planning strategies. Increased scrutiny from tax authorities, complex legal frameworks, the potential for misuse, and changes in tax laws are all factors that individuals should consider when utilizing offshore tax shelters. By understanding and addressing these risks, individuals can effectively harness the power of tax shelters while safeguarding their wealth legally.

Mitigating risks and ensuring legal compliance

When it comes to building wealth legally, it is essential to understand the importance of mitigating risks and ensuring legal compliance. As individuals, it is crucial to navigate the complex world of tax shelters and shell companies while staying within the boundaries of the law. This subchapter aims to provide valuable insights and strategies to help individuals protect their assets, optimize their tax planning, and maintain compliance with the relevant legal frameworks.

One of the key aspects of mitigating risks is understanding the legality of tax shelters and shell companies. While tax shelters can offer legitimate ways to reduce tax liabilities, it is crucial to distinguish between legal tax planning and illegal tax evasion. This subchapter will delve into the nuances of tax laws, helping individuals identify the fine line that separates tax optimization from illegal practices.

Moreover, offshore tax shelters have gained popularity among individuals seeking to preserve and grow their wealth. However, it is vital to understand the legal implications and compliance requirements associated with offshore tax shelters. This subchapter will equip individuals with the necessary knowledge to navigate the complexities of offshore tax shelters, ensuring they remain compliant with the laws of their home country and the jurisdictions where their assets are held.

Additionally, this subchapter will provide insights into the role of shell companies in wealth management. Shell companies can offer various benefits, including asset protection, privacy, and tax optimization. However, individuals must understand the legal and ethical considerations when utilizing shell companies. By exploring the legal compliance aspects, individuals can harness the power of shell companies while minimizing potential risks and avoiding legal pitfalls.

Mitigating risks and ensuring legal compliance also involves understanding the reporting and disclosure obligations associated with tax shelters and shell companies. This subchapter will outline the necessary steps individuals need to take to comply with the relevant reporting requirements, both domestically and internationally. By fulfilling these obligations, individuals can maintain transparency and mitigate the risk of legal consequences.

In conclusion, mitigating risks and ensuring legal compliance are integral components of building wealth legally through tax shelters and shell companies. By understanding the legal boundaries, compliance obligations, and ethical considerations, individuals can optimize their tax planning while staying on the right side of the law. This subchapter aims to empower individuals with the knowledge and tools they need to navigate this complex landscape successfully.

Impact of changing international tax regulations on offshore tax shelters

In recent years, the landscape of international tax regulations has undergone significant changes, impacting the viability and effectiveness of offshore tax shelters. These tax shelters, often used by individuals to mitigate their tax liabilities, have been subject to increased scrutiny and tighter regulations by tax authorities around the world. This subchapter delves into the impact of these changing regulations on offshore tax shelters and provides valuable insights for individuals seeking to navigate this evolving landscape.

The tightening of international tax regulations has been primarily driven by a global push for greater transparency and the prevention of tax evasion and money laundering. Governments worldwide have recognized the potential for abuse and the erosion of tax bases associated with offshore tax shelters. As a result, they have implemented measures to close loopholes and ensure that individuals are paying their fair share of taxes.

One significant change in the international tax arena is the implementation of the Common Reporting Standard (CRS). This global framework, developed by the Organisation for Economic Co-operation and Development (OECD), requires participating countries to exchange financial account information of their residents with other jurisdictions. The CRS aims to uncover hidden offshore assets and income, making it increasingly challenging for individuals to hide their wealth in tax havens.

Furthermore, governments have increased their efforts to crack down on tax shelter abuses by introducing stricter regulations and penalties. These measures include anti-avoidance rules, controlled foreign corporation (CFC) regulations, and general anti-abuse rules (GAAR). These regulations aim to prevent individuals from artificially shifting their income or assets offshore to avoid taxation.

The impact of these changing international tax regulations on offshore tax shelters is profound. Individuals who have relied on these structures to minimize their tax liabilities must now navigate a more complex and transparent environment. While offshore tax shelters may still offer legitimate tax planning opportunities, individuals need to ensure that their arrangements comply with the new regulations and do not fall into the realm of tax evasion.

In conclusion, the changing international tax regulations have significantly impacted the effectiveness and viability of offshore tax shelters. Individuals must be aware of these changes and adapt their tax planning strategies accordingly. By staying informed and seeking professional advice, individuals can continue to harness the power of tax shelters while remaining compliant with the evolving international tax landscape.

Chapter 9: Case Studies and Success Stories

Real-life examples of individuals benefiting from tax shelters

In today's complex financial landscape, individuals are always on the lookout for legal ways to minimize their tax burdens and increase their wealth. One effective strategy that has been successfully employed by many savvy investors is the use of tax shelters. These shelters, when used properly, can provide significant benefits and can help individuals build wealth legally. In this subchapter, we will explore some real-life examples of individuals who have benefited from tax shelters, providing inspiration and insight for those looking to follow in their footsteps.

One such example is John, a high-net-worth individual who owns multiple businesses. By setting up a carefully constructed offshore tax shelter, John was able to legally reduce his overall tax liability. By funneling a portion of his income through this tax shelter, he was able to take advantage of favorable tax laws in the foreign jurisdiction. As a result, John was able to reinvest a significant portion of his saved taxes back into his businesses, leading to exponential growth and increased wealth.

Another success story is that of Sarah, a real estate investor. Sarah used a tax shelter known as a 1031 exchange to defer capital gains taxes on the sale of her investment properties. By reinvesting the proceeds from the sale into similar properties, she was able to defer the tax liability indefinitely, allowing her to continue growing her real estate portfolio without the burden of immediate tax obligations. This strategy not only helped Sarah build wealth but also provided her with a steady stream of passive income.

In addition to these examples, there are countless others who have benefited from tax shelters in various ways. From entrepreneurs who have utilized captive insurance companies to protect their assets and reduce their tax liabilities to individuals who have set up self-directed IRAs to invest in alternative assets, the opportunities for tax savings and wealth accumulation are vast.

It is important to note that while tax shelters can be incredibly beneficial, they must be approached with caution and in compliance with all relevant tax laws. Seeking professional advice from tax experts and financial planners is essential to ensure that these strategies are implemented correctly and legally.

In conclusion, real-life examples of individuals benefiting from tax shelters demonstrate the immense potential for wealth accumulation and tax savings through these strategies. By understanding and utilizing the power of tax shelters, individuals can legally minimize their tax burdens and build their wealth in a sustainable manner.

Lessons learned from successful tax planning strategies

Tax planning is a crucial aspect of building wealth legally, and understanding successful strategies can help individuals make informed decisions to minimize their tax liabilities. In this subchapter, we will explore some key lessons learned from successful tax planning strategies that can benefit individuals seeking to optimize their financial situation.

1. Start Early: One of the most important lessons is to start tax planning early. By being proactive and aware of potential tax-saving opportunities, individuals can take advantage of various deductions, credits, and exemptions that can significantly reduce their tax burden. Planning ahead allows for strategic financial decisions that can maximize savings over the long run.

2. Seek Professional Advice: Tax laws are complex and constantly changing. It is essential to consult with a qualified tax professional who specializes in individual tax planning. They can help navigate the intricacies of tax

regulations, identify potential tax shelters, and provide personalized advice tailored to individual circumstances.

3. Understand Tax Shelters: Tax shelters are legal strategies that individuals can employ to minimize their tax liabilities. From retirement accounts, such as IRAs and 401(k)s, to investment vehicles like real estate, understanding the various tax shelters available is essential. By leveraging these shelters effectively, individuals can legally reduce their taxable income and grow their wealth.

4. Offshore Tax Shelters: Offshore tax shelters have gained attention for their potential benefits in minimizing tax obligations. However, it is crucial to approach offshore tax planning cautiously and within the bounds of the law. Individuals should be aware of the legal requirements, reporting obligations, and potential risks associated with offshore tax shelters.

5. Shell Companies: Another strategy often utilized in tax planning is the use of shell companies. These entities can provide certain advantages, such as asset protection and privacy, but their usage should be within legal boundaries. Understanding the legal frameworks surrounding shell companies is essential to avoid any legal consequences.

6. Stay Updated: Tax laws are subject to frequent changes, making it crucial for individuals to stay informed about the latest updates. Following reputable sources, attending seminars, and consulting with tax professionals can help individuals stay updated on the ever-evolving tax landscape. This knowledge empowers individuals to make informed decisions and optimize their tax planning strategies accordingly.

In conclusion, understanding the lessons learned from successful tax planning strategies is vital for individuals seeking to build wealth legally. By starting early, seeking professional advice, understanding tax shelters, offshore tax planning, and shell companies, individuals can navigate the complex tax landscape while minimizing their tax liabilities and maximizing their financial growth. Continuous education and staying updated on tax laws are key to ensuring successful tax planning strategies.

Inspiring stories of individuals who built wealth legally through tax shelters

Introduction:
In the world of finance and wealth management, tax shelters have long been a subject of intrigue and curiosity. Often misunderstood and associated with illegal activities, tax shelters can actually be powerful tools for individuals to legally reduce their tax burdens and build wealth. In this subchapter, we will explore inspiring stories of individuals who have successfully utilized tax shelters to their advantage, providing real-life examples and insights for our readers.

1. The Entrepreneurial Maverick:
Meet John, a self-made entrepreneur who started a small business in his early twenties. As his business grew, John realized the importance of optimizing his tax strategy to maximize his profits. Through careful research and consulting with tax professionals, he discovered the benefits of establishing a legitimate tax shelter, allowing him to reinvest his earnings back into his business and minimize his tax liability. Today, John's business thrives, and he serves as an inspiration for budding entrepreneurs looking to legally build wealth.

2. The Real Estate Mogul:
Susan had always been passionate about real estate. She started small, investing in residential properties and gradually expanding her portfolio. As she accumulated more properties, Susan realized the potential tax advantages of structuring her investments through a tax shelter. By utilizing legal strategies such as 1031 exchanges and real estate investment trusts (REITs), Susan was able to defer taxes on her gains and reinvest them into larger, more lucrative properties. Her success story demonstrates how individuals can build significant wealth through tax-advantaged real estate investments.

3. The Philanthropic Investor:

Robert, a successful executive, wanted to make a positive impact on society while minimizing his tax liability. He discovered the power of charitable trusts as a tax shelter, allowing him to donate appreciated assets while receiving substantial tax deductions. By establishing a charitable remainder trust, Robert was able to generate income for himself and his family during his lifetime, while ultimately leaving a significant philanthropic legacy. His story showcases how individuals can leverage tax shelters to create a win-win situation for both their financial goals and charitable aspirations.

Conclusion:

These inspiring stories of individuals who have legally built wealth through tax shelters illustrate the potential benefits and power of utilizing these strategies. By understanding the intricacies of tax law and working with knowledgeable professionals, individuals can navigate the complex world of tax shelters to optimize their financial growth while remaining compliant with regulations. These stories serve as a reminder that with the right knowledge and legal strategies, tax shelters can be valuable tools for individuals seeking to build wealth and secure their financial future.

Conclusion

Recap of key points discussed

In this subchapter, we will recap the key points discussed throughout the book "Building Wealth Legally: Harnessing the Power of Tax Shelters as an Individual." This book is specifically addressed to individuals who are interested in understanding the potential benefits of tax shelters and shell companies, along with offshore tax shelters for personal use. By recapping the essential points, we aim to provide a comprehensive overview for readers who are seeking a quick refresher or summary of the book's contents.

Throughout the book, we emphasized the importance of understanding the legal framework and guidelines surrounding tax shelters. It is crucial to operate within the boundaries of the law to avoid any potential legal repercussions. We discussed the different types of tax shelters available to individuals, including real estate investments, retirement accounts, and business deductions. Each of these strategies offers unique advantages and can significantly reduce tax liabilities for individuals.

Furthermore, we delved into the concept of shell companies and their role in tax planning. Shell companies can be utilized legally and ethically to protect assets, separate liabilities, and maximize tax benefits. However, it is important to note that the misuse of shell companies for illegal activities, such as money laundering or tax evasion, can lead to severe legal consequences.

Additionally, we explored the world of offshore tax shelters for individuals. Offshore accounts and investments can offer substantial tax advantages, asset protection, and increased privacy. However, we highlighted the importance of compliance with international tax laws and regulations, such as the Foreign Account Tax Compliance Act (FATCA). Non-compliance can result in hefty fines and penalties.

Throughout the book, we emphasized the significance of seeking professional advice from qualified tax experts and legal advisors. The constantly evolving tax laws and regulations make it essential to have a knowledgeable team to navigate the complexities of tax shelters and offshore structures.

In conclusion, "Building Wealth Legally: Harnessing the Power of Tax Shelters as an Individual" provides individuals with valuable insights into the world of tax shelters, shell companies, and offshore tax planning. By understanding the legal framework, seeking professional advice, and operating within the boundaries of the law, individuals can harness the power of tax shelters to build and protect their wealth.

Final thoughts on harnessing the power of tax shelters legally

In this subchapter, we will delve into the final thoughts on harnessing the power of tax shelters legally. Throughout this book, we have explored the different aspects of tax shelters, their benefits, and how individuals can take advantage of them to build wealth legally. It is important to remember that while tax shelters can be a valuable tool for reducing taxes, it is crucial to approach them with caution and within the boundaries of the law.

One of the key takeaways from this book is the importance of understanding the legal framework surrounding tax shelters. By being well-informed about the laws and regulations, individuals can navigate through the complexities of tax shelters without running afoul of any legal issues. This knowledge will provide individuals with the confidence to leverage tax shelters to their advantage while staying compliant with the applicable tax laws.

Another critical aspect is the need for transparency and proper documentation. When engaging in tax shelter strategies, individuals must maintain accurate records and be prepared to provide supporting documentation if required. This not only helps to substantiate the legitimacy of the tax shelter but also ensures compliance with reporting requirements. By keeping meticulous records, individuals can effectively demonstrate the legality and legitimacy of their tax shelter arrangements.

Furthermore, it is important to remember that tax shelters should not be the sole focus of an individual's financial strategy. While they can provide significant tax benefits, they should be part of a broader wealth-building plan. Diversifying investments, managing risk, and having a long-term perspective are equally essential for financial success.

Lastly, individuals should always seek professional advice when considering tax shelters. Consulting with tax professionals, accountants, or financial advisors who specialize in tax planning can provide valuable insights and guidance. These experts can help individuals navigate the complexities of tax laws, identify suitable tax shelters, and ensure compliance.

In conclusion, harnessing the power of tax shelters legally can be an effective strategy for individuals to build wealth. By understanding the legal framework, maintaining transparency, and seeking professional advice, individuals can leverage tax shelters while staying compliant with tax laws. Remember to approach tax shelters as part of a comprehensive financial plan and always be mindful of the broader goals of wealth creation and long-term financial security.

Encouragement and motivation for individuals to pursue wealth-building opportunities within the bounds of the law

In today's fast-paced world, where financial security is paramount, many individuals are seeking effective ways to build wealth legally. This subchapter aims to provide encouragement and motivation for individuals interested in exploring wealth-building opportunities within the bounds of the law. By harnessing the power of tax shelters as an individual, you can pave the way to financial success while ensuring compliance with legal regulations.

Tax shelters have long been recognized as valuable tools for wealth accumulation. However, it is crucial to understand that engaging in such endeavors must be done responsibly and ethically. By adhering to legal guidelines, you can maximize your financial growth while avoiding unnecessary risks.

Building wealth legally entails a comprehensive understanding of tax shelters and shell companies. This knowledge empowers individuals to make informed decisions and take advantage of the benefits offered by these strategies. By delving into the intricacies of tax shelters, you can optimize tax efficiency, protect your assets, and secure a brighter financial future.

Offshore tax shelters present another avenue for individuals seeking wealth-building opportunities. This subchapter aims to provide a comprehensive guide to offshore tax shelters for individuals. By exploring the benefits and risks associated with offshore tax shelters, you can make informed decisions that align with your financial goals. Whether it's asset protection, tax savings, or international investment opportunities, offshore tax shelters can offer unique advantages for individuals looking to expand their wealth.

It is important to note that while tax shelters and offshore strategies can be powerful wealth-building tools, they must be pursued within the bounds of the law. Engaging in illegal activities or attempting to evade taxes will not only lead to severe legal consequences but also tarnish your reputation and long-term financial prospects.

By adhering to legal guidelines and regulations, you can build wealth ethically and responsibly. This subchapter will provide you with the necessary knowledge and tools to navigate the complex world of tax shelters and offshore strategies, ensuring that you remain on the right side of the law.

Remember, building wealth legally is not only morally sound but also offers long-term stability and peace of mind. By leveraging the power of tax shelters and shell companies within legal boundaries, you can pave the way to financial prosperity while maintaining your integrity and reputation. Harness these opportunities, stay informed, and embark on a journey towards a prosperous future.